# A
# RHAPSODY
## OF POETIC WORDS
*A Treasured Gift From the Father Above*

## ELOUISE MATTHEWS

### FOREWORD BY
### STEPHANIE ANTOINETTE MATTHEWS

PRESS

# DEDICATION

This book is dedicated to children the world over, especially to those who have no parents, those who are suffering with a physical affliction, those who live in dire poverty and are deprived of education and proper nutrition, those children who are neglected by society only because of their race, national origin or social standing of their parents. Those children who live in a prosperous society yet are neglected by governments who seem to favor projects of status rather than caring for the neediest amongst us. Children are our future, and as a society, the outcome is predicated on the level of investment we make today. The greatest gift of God to humanity are our children. They are the reflection of who we truly are as humans. I am who I am because someone loved me and cared for me. May we continue to reach back always and make a child's life a better one.

# TABLE OF CONTENTS

### Section 4 An Intergenerational Legacy - Contending For The Faith

### Flourishing Like Palm Trees

# FOREWORD

"A Rhapsody of Poetic Words," is a collection of poetic words that will be a blessing to the young and old, men and women, boys and girls. Poetry is one of the oldest forms of literature. I think that it captures the emotions and expressions of the heart better than any other literary art form. As I read and edited my mother's manuscript, I was awe struck, deeply moved, and inspired by it. "Temptation Speaks," "Speak Truth to Emotions," and "Procrastination," resonated and gripped my soul. God wants us to trust Him and to trust His word.

I am a classical musician and a lover of many genres of music. My mother has written songs that encourage sinners as well as saints. These songs minister to our souls (mind, emotion, will). All throughout the songs, the Holy Spirit spoke to me. I've been lifted to rise, arise and go home, make up your mind to follow Christ, I have a living hope because of what Christ has done for me, and you can't take my dream from me. I began to weep and realized that the Holy

Spirit was encouraging me so that I could encourage other youth in my generation. This was a defining moment to purpose in my heart to walk righteous before God and before men and women in my generation. At that moment, I realized that God has given "new manna from heaven" to a new generation of believers.

The youth of today are looking for and seeking out role models that will inspire them to step out of the shadows of fear and self-doubt to do greatness during their life time on Earth. My mother has written biographical poems about the lives of godly men and women with multi-cultural and diverse racial backgrounds from all over the world, who have lived and some who still live among us. The youth of today know, have heard about, or read about some of them in school. Poetry allows my mother to express their lives in a profound artistic way. It's short, sweet, and rhythmic. In this book, parents, grandparents, and youth can read, listen, and learn about Mother Teresa, "A Sister," "A Mother," and "A Saint," "A Giant Slayer," and "The Soulful Symphony Music Ambassador," and many more men and women who are godly heroes for the younger generations today. Their lives are lights that spark hope, encouragement, and inspires them to live out the God-given vision for their lives.

Lastly, the final section in this book focuses upon the family. My mother reminds the reader, family, and the household of faith, to protect the godly legacy that God has given us. She calls it "an intergenerational legacy." I believe that the state of a nation is affected by the spiritual impact (or lack of it) mothers and fathers have had on their children. We cannot afford to allow the worldly godless culture to shape the lives of youth! I'm reminded that the first institution that God gave us after creating man in His own image was the family. This section is filled with blessings for the family: a prayer for the future generations, a blended family's commandments, and a completion of what my mom had started in her first book on commandments for the family. She has written blessings for daughters and sons as they prepare for marriage, and an e-mail message, which is one of the ways we communicate in the world today.

"A Rhapsody of Poetic Words," is a masterpiece and a great spiritual work of art. There will be times when God speaks to the youth in my generation, and I pray that they recognize His voice, be sensitive to the leading of the Holy Spirit, and heed His call and obey, Ecc. 12:1. If you desire your life to be enriched, I encourage you to read it and pay it forward by passing it on to bless others.

Stephanie A. Matthews
StringCandy.com

# ACKNOWLEDGEMENTS

I would like to thank God, my Heavenly Father, for the gift of His Word, the gift of His Son, and for the gift of imagination, creativity, and poetic words. Thank you Jesus Christ for being my Savior, Lord, and Life, and the Holy Spirit for being my teacher, comforter, and helper. I thank my husband, my personal consultant, who always assists me in bringing my books to life. A special thanks to my editor, Stephanie Matthews, my daughter, for her excellent writing and editing skills. We have communicated over the past several months until this manuscript was completed.

Thank you Mrs. Vivienne Anderson, a spiritual poet and excellent writer, for providing your comments and encouraging words. "The Giant Slayer" is a poem that has been dedicated to your husband, the late Bishop Vinton R. Anderson, who inspired me to write it. Thank you Mr. Patrick Lundy, an Ambassador of Music, for your comments and encouraging words. Thank you Mrs. Tuel, an authentic Christian educator, who has been my mentor, and a beloved friend for thirty-eight years. The Holy Spirit encouraged me to bless you and I obeyed! I thank my family, sister, brother, friends, and prayer partners for their support: Cheryl Matthews, Isaac Matthews, Edith Young, Louis Brandy, Cheryl McAfee Mitchell, Rosalind Baylor, Beverly William Cleaves, Ife Johnson, Helen Hannah, Linda Smith, Isis Tuel, Elaine Williams, Leonor Greenidge, Juanita Douglas, Alexis Weaver, Penelope White, Aree Scott, Joyce Parker, Betty Ross, and Shermaine Waldon.

A special thanks to all of the churches and pastors who have contributed to my spiritual growth and development: Sequell Baptist ( the late Pastor Gaines), the church that I grew up in, Ebenezer AME (Pastor Grainger Browning and Pastor Jo Ann Browning) the church that my family grew up in, and Mt. Ennon Baptist (Pastor Delman Coates), my home church. I thank God for my spiritual teachers of the word of God: Pastor Delman Coates, Bishop Jackie McCullough, Pastor Nike Wilheims, Pastor Charles Stanley, Pastor John Bisagno, Pastor Kenneth Hagin Sr., Pastor Adrian Rogers, Pastor Myles Munroe Sr., Apostle Michael Youssef, Bishop T.D. Jakes, and Archbishop Duncan Williams. What a Mighty God we serve! Finally, I thank Phillis Wheatley, Maya Angelou, Nikki Giovanni, Eloise Greenfield, and Helen Steiner Rice for blazing a poetic trail for others to follow.

# INTRODUCTION

A Rhapsody of Poetic Words will inspire, enlighten, uplift, provoke, instruct, and give you hope. Inside the covers of this book are blessings that await the reader. They include poems, songs, family commandments, and other poetic expressions to bless the reader, their families, friends, and the body of Christ.

The purpose of this book is to empower believers to become blessings to those in Christ as well as to those without Christ. The Lord said to Peter in His word in Luke 22:32, "after you have been converted, strengthen your brothers," and this in essence is what I've been compelled to do with the poetic gift that God has given to me. We are epistles of Christ with the spirit of the living God within us, 2 Cor. 3:2-3.

Why did I write this book, you might be thinking? Well, I wrote this book to give to you and the world what God has given to me. The light of Christ has shined in my heart and the power of God is working in me, 2 Cor. 4:6-7. God calls us to be faithful and productive stewards over the gift(s) that He has given us. God gives us gifts to fulfill His purpose/assignment for our lives. I refuse to die with it! I refuse to allow procrastination to rob you of the blessings that God has given to me to deliver to you! I am determined to invest my talent into the kingdom of heaven until the Master returns. As Christians, we must be intentional about blessing others with our God-given gift.

Lastly, this book was written to remind godly mothers, godly fathers, godly grandmothers, godly grandfathers, godly aunts, godly uncles, and godly guardians to pass on a spiritual legacy to the future (younger) generations.

God is raising up a ruling government of the kingdom of Heaven on Earth who will think the way He thinks because they have the mind of Christ, and walk in the power and authority that Christ has invested in them. I invite you the reader to open up "A Rhapsody of Poetic Words," and become inspired, enlightened, and motivated to share it with your mothers, fathers, sons, daughters, grandmothers, grandfathers, grandsons, granddaughters, friends, and with the body of Christ. Heavenly Father, I pray that you would use this gift of poetic words to strengthen your people to become living epistles that will be read by their families, friends, and the world. Grant to them the spirit of wisdom, revelation, and the knowledge of You. Enlighten their minds to comprehend and receive the glorious and great inheritance that has been given to them as a joint heir with Jesus Christ. Let your kingdom come on Earth in each one of their lives, in Jesus's Mighty Name, A-men.

# A RHAPSODY OF POETIC WORDS

My heart overflows with a Rhapsody of Poetic Words,
Shining light on the blank pages of life,
With every breath, you impart life to me,
Causing me to walk in the light of truth,
And granting me a coat of many colors.

I take back my spiritual authority,
Because of the power Christ invested in me,
Breaking the chains of bondage to walk into freedom.
Lord restore your glory in me.
I weep openly over the loss of love ones,
'Cause I know it's part of the faith journey of life,
Remembering this season has a short life span,
I anticipate joy, and when it comes,
I sing the universal song of life.

My heart overflows with a Rhapsody of Poetic Words,
Rejoicing over mentors and guardian angels
And a new generation of believers
Contending for the faith,
And spreading the gospel of Christ,
Keepers of a glorious legacy,
Safe under God's banner of love,
Anchored securely in Jesus Christ,
And safe under His blood.
Lord, my heart overflows with
A Rhapsody of Poetic Words!

# TUNING INTO THE MIND OF CHRIST

# IN THE MASTER POET'S HAND

I am a poem in the master poet's hand,
He is the voice which guides me
Along the pages of life,
Birthing rhyme and rhythm,
A voice ever flowing in my ear.

He breathes words that give me life
On the blank pages before me,
Who speaks power to each word uttered,
That gives shape and form to me,
A simple poem created in the master poet's hand.

# LORD, DEPOSIT YOUR LIFE IN ME

Lord, deposit your life in me,
Wash me and make me anew,
With your spirit divine,
Your word in my heart,
Your truth in my soul,
And your very breath.

Lord, deposit your life in me,
Transform and make me anew,
Pour in your healing oil,
Blessings, hope, and grace,
Your joy, peace, and revelation,
With your love and unshakeable faith.

Lord, deposit your life in me,
As I go in Jesus's name,
To carry the Good News of Christ,
To reach the lost and heal the sick,
Bring deliverance to the bound,
All with your spirit divine.

Lord, deposit your life in me,
Anoint me and make me anew,
Put your word in my heart,
Your truth in my soul,
And your very breath,
All with your spirit divine,
Lord, deposit your life in me.

# THE FATHER'S CALLING FOR OUR LIVES

Each of us has a God-given calling on our life,
To bring life and not death into the world,
To nurture the lives of the young and old,
To protect, rescue, and defend life,
To rise up as blood bought soldiers,
To fight against pharaoh's decrees,
Refusing to bow down or obey his orders.

We must use our God-given calling and power to oppose
The oppressor, by using our voices to speak up and speak out
Against racial and economic inequality, and injustice.
To tell the oppressor "no" and to tell God "yes,"
To use our hands to uplift our brothers here and abroad,
Use our feet to march and stand together as sons of the Most High King,
To walk in the light of truth found in God's Holy and Righteous Word.

We must choose to work for God
And walk in His high calling for our lives,
To be helpers, not hurters, of our brothers
In our homes and across the land.

We must remain true to our calling,
By bringing forth life and not death,
To protect life and not crush life,
To walk in faith, and fight the good fight of faith.
To rise up, stand up, step out, step up
To protect, rescue, and defend the lives of our brothers.

We have been called to team up with God
To give life , uplift life, and protect life
Because God, our Heavenly Father
Has given us this calling.
A-men, A-men, A-men!

# TAKE BACK YOUR SPIRITUAL AUTHORITY

Men of God, take back your spiritual authority,
Press your way to Jesus!
Pray earnestly and persistently against demonic
bystanders
Who have blocked your way,
Keeping you from getting to Jesus.
Rise up and climb up into your heavenly places
with Christ,
Who is seated on high.

Pray, praise, and worship the Most High God
Until He empowers you with strength, power,
and might.
Receive ye keys to the kingdom of God
To bind and loose and walk in your authority,
Conquering fears and strongholds,
Asking God to cast your sins and the forefathers' sins
Into the sea of forgetfulness.

Climb up onto the mountaintop, walking in supernat-
ural power.
Receive ye the promise from God, the Father, on High.
As you tarry, He will meet you there, so fervently pray,
Then rise up and do battle in the heavenlies,
Putting the enemy under your feet,
Taking your position of authority.
Use God's Word, your weapon, to take back what has
been stolen.
Don't wave the white flag of defeat,
Just stand up, rise up, and climb up
And take back your spiritual authority!

# THE MESSAGE OF THE CROSS

The first Adam gave us life on Earth,
But Jesus gave us power to live life abundantly
on Earth
And eternal life in heaven,
So we can be in the world
And not of this world!
Jesus was God on Earth,
And we too are the Kingdom of God
On Earth!

So remember, no man can ever
Do the finished work that Jesus
Has done for you and for me.
Christ demonstrated agape love for His enemies too,
A new way For God's children to live on Earth.
My dearly beloved, understand
The message of the cross.

# WHERE THERE IS A WILL THERE'S A WAY

Where there is a will, there's a way,
A way out of troubles into triumph,
A way out of mourning into joy,
A way out of the earthly realm into the heavenly realm,
A way out of the kingdom of darkness
Into the kingdom of light,
Because where there is a will there's a way.

Where there is a will there's a way,
A way out of sorrow into joy,
A way out of sickness into health,
A way out of poverty into prosperity,
A way out of the flood into the ark of safety,
A way out of bondage into freedom,
Because where there is a will, there's a way.

Where there is a will, there's a way,
A way out of the pit into the palace,
A way out of despair into hope,
A way out of sin into salvation
A way out of doubt into faith,
Because where there is a will there's a way.

Where there is a will there's a way,
A way out of spiritual death into eternal life,
A way out of generational curses into generational
blessings,
A way out of the valley of defeat
Onto the mountain top of victory,
Because where there is a will,
Praise God, there's a way.

# TEMPTATION SPEAKS

If you want fame or a big name,
To be known in the eyes of men,
And you desire the glitter and glamour,
Let me take you there.

If you want a spouse or a house
To showcase from here to there,
With beauty and servants and things,
Then let me take you there.

If you want to fan the flames of passion
And pleasure that leaps from flesh to flesh,
And travels the seas in love boats and yachts,
Then let me take you there.

If you want riches, diamonds, wealth, and power
That this world has to give,
To store up in vaults and world banks,
Then let me take you there,
Just let ME take you there!

# PROCRASTINATION

A spirit that speaks
Persuading you to delay
Your today, "til tomorrow,"
Whispering to you "What's the rush,
There's time … tomorrow."

A sly cunning spirit
And an enemy to your todays,
It will cause you to funeralize your dreams
By robbing you of your time,
Because time is a spiritual battleground,
Of God and Satan.

A deceptive polite voice,
That will tempt you to hesitate,
Weaken your will,
Communicates with your emotions,
Keeping you from persevering
To complete the race,
And even cause you not to receive
God's rewarding words of
"Well done thy good and faithful servant."

# SPEAK TRUTH TO EMOTIONS

At times, I might feel unworthy, but I have great worth,
For Christ died for me,
I am highly valued and loved by God,
That's why He created me!

At times, I might feel lowly,
But I'm a joint heir with Jesus Christ,
I'm seated together with Him,
And I've been given all spiritual
Blessings in heavenly places.

At times, I might feel like a victim,
But I'm more than a conqueror and overcomer,
The greater one is within me,
And I have been given life more abundantly.

At times, I might feel lonely,
Yet, I'm never alone,
My Heavenly Father is with me always,
And He abides deep within.

At times, I might feel defeated,
But I can do all things through Christ,
Who gives me the strength,
And I walk in victory and success.

And so, I speak truth to my soul,
When my feelings try to take control,
And dictate to my emotions to travel the wrong road,
So that my mind stands upon what it knows.

# WEEP, MY CHILD, WEEP

Weep, my child, weep,
It's a cleansing, purging process,
Weep, my child, weep,
Release the pain, sorrow, and grief
All at Jesus's feet,
For God has a brighter day
For you tomorrow.

Weep, my child, weep,
To receive tenderness of heart,
That softens to feel love
And compassion for others,
So, weep my child, weep.

# LIFE

Life is a see saw,
Which end are you on?
Are you rising, in faith, in life,
And growing and maturing in Christ?
Or are you descending
And sinking deep in sin,
And crawling on the ground floor
Of defeat in life?

# THE FAITH JOURNEY

Foster your faith in God for your faith journey,
Rid yourself of weight that will weigh you down
And move forward fearlessly in faith.
Let prayer map out your destination route,
And be in constant communication with the Master.

Allow the Holy Spirit, your guide and advocate,
To direct you on the righteous path
As He makes the crooked path straight.
Watch out for pitfalls and road blocks,
Look to the One who's seated on high,
He'll be your shade and hiding place.
Take God's Holy Word, your compass,
Nourishment, and shining light all along the way.

Keep your eyes focused upward, respond rightly.
As you pass through the wilderness
And grow tired and weary,
Encourage yourself "I've come too far to quit!"
Keep moving on your faith journey in Christ,
And each day given is to prepare you for eternity,
As you stay in position to transition
To your Heavenly Home in Glory.

# OH AFRICA

Oh Africa, what has happened
To the ancient of days?
Will those days ever return?
Oh my dark skinned kinsmen,
Will life ever be as they were
In the ancient of days?
When our spirits were in tune
With the Creator God,
And our hearts were filled
With love for our fellow man,
And our minds fashioned things
To bless and uplift mankind?

Oh Africa, how our youth
Needs to live in a world like
The ancient of days,
A world where freedom, love, and peace abound;
Instead, they are tossed about
In a cruel and loveless world.
Oh Africa, will there ever be a rebirth
Of the ancient of days,
Or will it forever be a thing of the past,
Remembered in history
As the ancient of days.

# A WELCOME ADDRESS

Good Morning Church and praise God on this glorious Palm Sunday! Ecclesiastes 3:1 tells us that "to everything there is a season, and a time to every purpose under the heaven." We thank God for this season of rebirth, His new mercies, His Amazing Grace, and Everlasting Love that He has showered upon each of us on this day! On behalf of our Pastor ... and the body of Christ..., whose lives are built up in the Word of God, we welcome our visitors, family, and friends to the house of God. The Holy Spirit welcomes you too. Just as nature obeys the voice of God and declares the Glory of God, let us also obey God by loving and forgiving each other, building each other up in the faith, strengthening, and serving one another as God has commanded us to do (Gal. 5:13, 1 Thes. 5:11)). Our pastor wants you to know that we all must spring forward in believing and trusting God! So take off your winter coats of sin, burdens, fears, and doubt, and put on your spring clothes of trust, faith, joy, righteousness, and freedom, and walk into a life of victory! Put on the Mind of Christ. That's the greatest garment that you could ever wear! We want you to know that you are in the right place among the people of God who don't mind clapping and waving their hands and saying "Yes Lord" and "A-Men!" If birds can sing praises to our God then so can we! We don't mind dancing, shouting, and praising God, because we know that He alone is worthy of all praises! God woke us up this morning, and He gave us this day to bless His Holy and Righteous Name!

So welcome my beloved, and please allow the love of God to shine into your souls and give you a rebirth in your spirits as you experience the people of God rejoicing and glorifying God .... on this Palm Sunday. We don't want you to go back home the same way that you left! If the Winter season has moved over for Spring, then sin has to move over for salvation, and sadness has to move over for rejoicing, and doubt has to move over for faith. We decree and declare these things in your lives on this Palm Sunday. Again, we welcome you into the house of God, among the people of God here at ...!

# COME ON CHILDREN, LET'S SING!

# A MUSICAL NOTE

I am a musical note in the universal song of life.
I help to make up the hallelujah song,
That fills the heavenly atmosphere,
Giving glory and honor to the Creator God
That angels stop, pause, and listen to.

# TAKE A LOOK AROUND MY BROTHER, MY SISTER

Take a look around my brother, my sister,
People are in need of a helping hand,
There's violence across the land,
Children are dying before they get a chance to live.

Take a look around my brother, my sister,
People are searching for shelter,
Fleeing to and fro on foot, wherever they can.

Take a look around my brother, my sister,
There's police brutality in the black community,
Inflicted upon young black boys and girls,
Just because of their hue.
Mothers are crying because their children are dying,
And conforming to this world's culture.

Take a look around my brother, my sister,
Lord knows we're in need of a helping hand
To deliver us from evil
That's spreading across the land.

Just take a look around my brother, my sister,
Can't you see we're in need of a Saviour,
To rescue us from the troubles of this world?
Only a Saviour's hand can deliver us,
Like no other can.
Just take a look around my brother, my sister.

# STANDING ON LEVEL GROUND

"We are standing on level ground at the foot of the
cross." [1]
Inspite of our failures and short comings,
Jesus loved us enough to die for us all.
We are standing on level ground at the foot of the cross.
For Jesus shed his blood for us all.
Yes, we are standing on level ground at the foot of
the cross.

Jesus took on our sins as He hung on that cross.
We are standing on level ground at the foot of the cross,
Jesus took on an earth garment to experience our trials
And temptations.

Oh thank you God for level ground, level ground.
Oh thank you Heavenly Father for level ground,
level ground
At the foot of the cross.

The word of God says in John 3:16
"For God so loved the world
That He gave His only begotten son,
That whosoever believeth in Him
Should not perish, but have everlasting life."

Church, Jesus invited "whosoever believes"
To come to Him,
And the good news of the gospel is,

---

[1]    Pastor Delman Coates, sermon quote delivered to Mt. Ennon
       Church Congregation, Clinton, MD. December 2015

We are all standing on level ground
At the foot of the cross.

Come on down and stand
At the foot of the cross.
Come on down and stand
At the foot of the cross.

Sinner man, there's salvation
At the foot of the cross,
Sinner man, there's cleansings
At the foot of the cross.

Sinner man, there's deliverance
At the foot of the cross.
We are all standing on level ground
At the foot of the cross.

Holy Spirit, lead me to stand on level ground,
At the foot of the cross.
Lead me dear Lord, to stand on level ground,
At the foot of the cross.

# LIFTED TO RISE

Because Christ has power to heal,
His reputation has spread across the land.
Many come to hear and be healed,
Some increasing in faith, and others – "bystanders,"
But the power of the Lord is real and present to heal.

God's word tells us of some brothers who
Brought a paralyzed brother lying on
His bed of affliction to see Jesus.
They lifted him carrying his burden before the Lord,
When he could not carry himself. (Luke 5:18-20)

Thank God for lifting,
My brothers, thank you for lifting me,
Thank you for lifting me.
Oh thank you for lifting me.

Yet they couldn't get to Jesus,
Because of the multitude surrounding Him.
The door was blocked and they couldn't enter in.
But, inspite of this, they lifted (up) and carried
Their brother's burden,
Even though they could not reach Jesus.
Thank you God for burden bearers
And heavy load sharers.
For they lifted their brother,

Pressing their way to Jesus,
Climbing and rising in faith,
Reaching the housetop carrying their brother.

For the power of the Lord was real
And present to heal those who were lifted
In faith and in their bodies.
And Jesus looked up, seeing the brothers' faith
And the brother being lifted and spoke a word,
Lifting his sins and healing his body.

Thank you God for lifting,
Oh my brother, thank you for lifting me,
Thank you for lifting me,
Oh thank you for lifting me,
So that I can arise and begin anew.

Thank you for carrying me,
Thank you for loving me,
And oh my brothers, thank you for lifting me
And bringing me to the Master,
So that I can arise and begin anew again.

# I WILL ARISE AND GO HOME

If ever you journey to a far country,
And spend all your earnings and money
On thrills and frills,
And there's none left to obtain shelter,
Or a place to lay your weary head,
Tell your soul to arise and go home.

If ever you find yourself in want or need,
And your body is weak from hunger or thirst,
And your so-called friends forsake thee,
Tell your soul to arise and go home.

If ever you are drowning in deep despair,
And wallowing in foolish choices and worldly
pleasures,
And your heart is lonely and far, far from home,
And you can't see your father's face nor hear his voice,
Tell your soul to arise and go home.

I will arise and go home,
I will arise and go home,'
Oh my soul, I will arise and go home.

I will arise and go home,
I will arise and go home,
Oh my soul, I will arise and go home.

God's love can find you
And draw you back to Him,
And you will arise and go home. (Spoken word –
speak aloud this last stanza)

# LORD I'VE DECIDE TO FOLLOW YOU

I've tried to walk independently of you,
Followed the crowd and lost my way.
…Stumbling and falling and straying
From the path that leads to you.
I've become part of the world
And have been led astray,
So Lord, I've decided to follow you.

I've been mocked, misunderstood, and falsely
accused,
And really wish to explain.
…Felt the pain of emotional rejection,
Yet in my heart I desire you.
…Friends are few, oh so few,
But your presence and hand continuously
Shows me the righteous way,
So Lord, I've decided to follow you.

Lord I pray for the persecutors,
And the persecuted too,
Who have done no wrong,
Yes, I see the light and path that leads to you,
And I'm ready to stand for you,
So Lord, I've decided to follow you.

Lord, I'm ready to stand for you,
So I've decided to follow you.
Lord I'm ready to stand for you,
So I've decided to follow you,
Because you will never let me down.

For I see the light and path
That leads to you,
And in my heart, I desire you,
And I'm ready to stand for you,
So Lord, I've decided to follow you,
Because you will never, ever let me down.

# CROSS OVER TO THE OTHER SIDE

Lord I've been travelling through this world of sin,
Your map I've read and Guide I've followed,
As you commanded the sun from the east to come,
Cross over to the other side.

Lord, since a child I've searched for you,
And you did not hide,
From the south came goodness and mercy fol-
lowing me,
I've heard your voice and seen your (divine) light,
Directing me on my way,
Cross over to the other side.

All throughout my youthful years,
I've travelled this narrow road,
Refusing to veer off on the broad one,
Or deviate from the righteous path,
And you granted me patience
In the heat of the day,
Seeing a glimpse of a harvest and
The north star up ahead,
In the distance gave me hope,
That I will cross over to the other side.

Lord I've been travelling through this world of sin,
I've grown tired and weary,
But in my golden years,
Lord you have sustained and cared for me,
The sun appears in the western horizon,
As I've come to the end of the line,

I'm ready to cross over to the other side,
Lord, I'm ready to cross over to the other side.

Lord I'm ready,
Yes I'm ready,
Lord, I'm ready,
Yes, I'm ready,
Lord, I'm ready,
Yes, I'm ready,
Lord I'm ready to cross over
To the other side.

# A LIVING HOPE

I have a living hope,
Because of what Christ has done for me,
For He conquered death, hell, and the grave.
I have a Saviour who's triumphed over man's fall,
And Jesus's death took care of it all.

I have a living hope,
Because Christ paid the price for sin,
So that you and I can live again,
Just as I know when the cold winter ends,
The warmth of spring will come again.

I have a living hope that my trials cannot exceed
The strength He's given me to bear them,
And I can cast my cares upon Him,
And my prayers will unlock heaven's storehouse
Where boundless treasures reside.

I have a living hope, an unshakeable hope of glory
Because I have Christ within,
And I can rise above everything that
Tries to weigh me down.

I have a living hope,
Because I have testimonies of victories in this life,
I serve a promise keeping, changeless God
Who will grant me eternal and everlasting life,
And there's a crown of righteousness laid up for me.

I have a living hope,
That when I die, heaven is my eternal home,
A reserve inheritance for you and for me.
Praise be to God the Father
Who has given us a living hope,
A glorious anchor for our souls.

# A FRESH RAIN

When my life is filled with drought and barrenness,
And I thirst and hunger for you,
Lord, send the rain,
Let it saturate my heart
And let a stream of fresh flowing
Water wash over me.

When death hovers over my life's dream,
And my vision seems to slowly fade,
Lord send the rain,
Let it saturate my heart,
And let the stream of fresh flowing
Water wash over me.

When the reservoir and indwelling stream runs low,
And my life ceases to produce fruit,
Lord send the rain,
Let it saturate my heart,
Let a stream of fresh flowing
Water wash over me.

When my life becomes polluted with worldly
influences,
And mine eyes focus away from you,
Lord send the rain,
Wash my mind with your word
To remove the world's filth and stains,
Let the stream of fresh flowing
Water wash over me.

Lord send the rain,
Let a refreshing rain shower down from heaven above,
To revive my thirsty soul,
Lord send the cooling rain during the heat of the day,
To cause my soul adrift to shift toward you again.
Lord send the rain to cause fruit to spring forth,
So a harvest can be produced in my life again,
Lord send the rain,
Let it saturate my heart
And let the stream of fresh flowing water
Wash, wash over me.

Send it Lord send it,
Let the rain clouds form,
And send the rain.
Send it Lord, send it,
Let the rain clouds form
And send it Lord, send it.

Lord send the rain,
Let it saturate my heart,
Let the stream of fresh flowing water
Wash, wash over me
To revive my soul again.

Send the rain,
A fresh flowing rain
To saturate my heart
And revive my soul again,
Lord, send the rain.

# LORD SHINE ON ME

Lord when I can't see my way,
And I don't know which way to go,
Don't allow pride or anxiety to cloud my view,
Let your light shine on the path I must take,
Allow your truth to shed light on my sin,
Shine your light Lord.

When my heart has grown cold from heartbreak,
And from wandering in a loveless world,
Send a flame to rekindle the fire within,
To let the flame of love burn brightly again,
Lord, let Your Son fill my day
As I look to The Way, The Truth, The Light,
Shine your light Lord.

Turn not your face from me,
Like a child who's strayed from his mother
In a candy store,
Lord it's your face (that) I must see,
And to know that it's okay,
Shine, shine, shine on me.

Spirit of the living God,
Dispel all darkness in my soul,
And shadows cast across my path,
As I meditate upon thy word,
And await your finished work,
Shine, shine, shine on me.
Shine your light on me.
I want to know that you're watching me,

That you love and care for me,
Lord, let your face shine brightly upon me.

Oh, oh, oh
Shine on me
Yes Lord
Shine on me.

Oh, oh, oh
Shine on me
Yes Lord
Shine on me.

Oh, oh, oh
Shine on me
Yes Lord
Shine on me.

Spirit of the living God,
Dispel all darkness in my soul,
And shadows cast across my path,
Then rekindle love deep within my heart,
And let your light
Shine, shine, shine on me.

# A SEASON TO SHINE

This is your season to shine, shine, shine.
This is your moment to shine, shine, shine.
This is your hour to shine, shine, shine.

God said, your time of preparation has ended,
You have labored to achieve your dream.
You believed God and took the faith walk,
And it's your time to shine, shine, shine.

You have entered into a season of reaping
The harvest for the seeds that have been planted
In the fertile soil of your life,
And it's your time to shine, shine, shine.

This is your moment to shine, shine, shine,
You have believed the word of God,
And stood on His promises for your life,
And now your season to shine has come,
Praise to the Almighty God,
This is your season to shine, shine, shine.

Glory to God in the Highest
This is your season to shine, shine, shine,
Give thanks to the King of Kings
For bringing you into this season,
This moment and this hour,
To shine, shine, shine.

# A MIGHTY SAVIOR

Have you been held captive because of a sin?
Is an addiction or emotional wound inflicting your soul
And keeping you bound?
Is sins of the flesh weighing heavily upon your heart?
Then be encouraged my brother, my sister,
Jesus, the Lord God Almighty is mighty to save.

Has the world engulfed you and stripped you of your
identity?
And you don't know right from wrong,
And can't tell night from day and you stand at
hell's gate?
Then take heart my brother, my sister,
Jesus, the Lord God Almighty is mighty to save.

Are you distant from God because of broken promises,
And distrust, and you've suffered much hurt and pain,
Because of family members and so-called (fake)
friends?
Then take heart my brother, my sister,
Jesus, the Lord God Almighty is mighty to save.

Jesus wants to be your Savior and take your sins away,
Just believe in Him and let Him set you free.
You can trust Him for He will not disappoint you,
Because Jesus, the Lord God Almighty is mighty
to save,
He is mighty to save, Jesus is mighty to save.
Jesus, the Lord God Almighty is mighty to save.

He alone can forgive sin,
He came to save, not condemn,
For He knows the world we live in,
He is mighty to save.
Jesus wants to be your Savior,
And He loves you unconditionally,
He is mighty to save,
Jesus, the Lord God Almighty is mighty to save,
He is mighty to save.

# LORD, I TAKE YOU AT YOUR WORD

Lord, my faith is in your Holy Word,
And I must increase in the knowledge of you.
I submit and humbly walk in your presence,
And stand in awe of you.

Lord, I release my faith,
Through prayer, as I stand upon your word,
Laying claim to every promise and confess it,
As you respond in a miraculous way.

I daily walk in the believer's authority,
And in the mighty power in me that worketh,
As the Holy Spirit gives me power and confidence
To walk in victory.

Lord, my faith rest in your Holy Word,
And I believe every word is true,
Renewing my mind daily (with your word),
As you sanctify and purify,
Causing me to bear spiritual fruit.

Activating mountain moving faith,
Be thou removed I speak,
Casting them (this and that) into the sea,
Doubting not, growing stronger
With a faith centered in Thee.

Lord, I draw nigh to Thee,
As you draw closer to me,
Inhabiting every praise,
As I bless your Holy Name!

I believe it,
I believe it,
Lord, I believe every word is true.

I believe it,
I believe it,
Lord, I believe every word is true,
And it impacts all of me (in a spiritual way),
And I stand secure in it.

Lord, I submit and humbly walk in your presence,
As I stand in awe of You.
For my faith rest in your Holy Word,
And I must increase in the knowledge of You.

So I believe it,
I believe it,
And lay claim to every promise and confess it,
All because Lord, I believe every word is true. (say
this line slowly)

# THE COAT OF MANY COLORS

Lord, give me a coat of many colors,
" A coat of salvation, a coat of Christian character,
And a coat of an overcomer." [2]

Lord give me a coat of many colors,
A coat of salvation, a free gift from God,
For Christ's sake for you and for me.
And a coat of Christian character,
Work on me Lord and help me to stand for
righteousness.

Lord, as I walk by faith, go through,
My tests and trials in life, love and forgive,
Then Lord, grant to me a coat of an overcomer.

Lord, thank You for giving me the coat
Of salvation, a free gift that wasn't earned.
Thank you Lord for giving me the coat
Of Christian character as I pass these
Tests in life,
And by faith, I know that I will receive
A coat of an overcomer.

As I travel this world of sin,
Grant to me the power and strength
To resist and denounce sin
And demonstrate the light of Christ
And the power that works within.

[2]  Pastor Jentezen Franklin, '"How to Be an Overcomer"
sermon, Free Chapel Worship, Gainsville, GA. May 1, 2016.

Glory to God in the Highest for
Granting me the coat of Christian character.
Praise God, my Heavenly Father,
Thank you for weaving together for me
A coat of many colors.

All praise to the Omniscient, Omnipotent, and
Omnipresent God,
Who has offered salvation to all
Who would believe and receive.
And as I travel through this world of sin,
Give me the power and strength to pass every test,
And manifest a changed life by the power that
worketh within.
Glory to God, my Heavenly Father, who will
grant to me
A coat of Christian character.

And Father in Heaven above, in all things, help me
to give thanks,
As I go through adversities and surrender all,
Standing on your Holy Word, and prayer,
And walking by faith.
Lord, for I know You will grant to me
A coat of an overcomer.
For I will walk as an overcomer
And demonstrate the light of Christ
And a life that has been changed
By the power of His Mighty Word
That worketh deep within.
Thank you Heaven Father,
For granting the coat of many colors.

# LORD RESTORE ME IN YOUR GLORY

Lord restore me in your glory,
All consuming fire, set ablaze in my heart,
Burn up every sinful and evil thought,
Holy Spirit, soften this stony heart,
Make ready for your Holy Word.
Fill me up until there's no desire for
The pleasures of sin.

Lord restore me in your glory,
All consuming fire,
Destroy every idol in my heart,
Let my heart long for you and you only,
Jesus, I seek intimacy with you,
Drive away the ungodly,
Point me to others who desire you too.
Holy Spirit, set afire in my heart,
Fill me with your power,
For I'm washed in Jesus's blood.

Lord, restore me in your glory,
Let a conversion take place in my soul
So I can rule over sin
And walk in my royal priesthood.
Make me a vessel of honor,
And my temple holy.
Fill me with Holy Ghost fire
As I feast upon Your Word,
Make me a lover of Truth,
With a will to walk in righteousness,
And praise your Holy Name.

Restore me Lord, restore me,
Restore me in your glory.
Restore me Lord, restore me,
Restore me in your glory.

# Keeping In Step With The Master

# A Defining Moment

A Moment in Time
Given to Deliver
God's Plan
To Mankind

# A MENTOR

A brother's keeper
Mother, father, coach, teacher
Passer of the baton,
Your guardian angel.

# A CHRISTIAN EDUCATOR

To guide and teach children the godly way,
To fulfill dreams, visions, and purpose in life;
Ordained by God to faithfully serve,
For a righteous reward God will pay.

To uplift a new generation of youth,
To educate the minds to moral truth,
And leave behind a legacy of love,
That leads children to the Father above.

Fosters relationships with parents, moms, and dads,
And invites them to be part of the school team,
To encourage the youth God entrusted in their care,
As their children climb to reach their dreams.

A leader, a servant, and a godly teacher,
In partnership with the Heavenly Father,
To deliver the message of truth,
To the youth and colleagues too,
Because God needed someone, he decided to
create you.
(Written in honor of Penelope White)

# CHOSEN TO BE A NATION BUILDER

You were chosen to be a Nation Builder,
To help build and shape a thriving nation of youth,
To help transform their minds into believers,
And to hold God's Word as true.

You were chosen to be a Nation Builder,
To train, educate, and inspire God's youth,
From the tallest to the smallest,
To believe that they can achieve to succeed,
And accomplish the dreams and visions,
Deep within their hearts.

God granted you divine favor from on high,
As you grew in your faith and His amazing grace,
To love, teach, and educate with patience,
Until they caught hold of their future;
You were faithful to the call,
That's why God chose you for this mission.
(Written in honor of Aree Scott)

# GOD'S PRAISE AND WORSHIP TEAM

The praise and worship team teaches us
How to praise and worship Christ our Lord,
Fixing their eyes only upon Him,
Creating an atmosphere that welcomes Jesus.
Allowing God to release His power to heal,
Deliver, bless, destroy yokes – setting captive free,
God's true praisers and worshipers.
So put on a garment of praise,
And lift the spirit of heaviness.

The praise and worship team exalts
And proclaims God's goodness and greatness,
Magnifying the Lord who dwells in shekinah glory,
Inviting Emmanuel into our midst,
As they lift up Christ The Lord,
Invoking Him to draw us unto Himself.
God's true praisers and worshipers.
So put on a garment of praise,
And lift the spirit of heaviness.

The praise and worship team's hearts and minds,
Are corporately focused upon the Lord,
Ushering us into His presence,
Surrendering all, and loving Him,
Uttering melodies from their hearts
With high praise upon their lips,
Yielding to the Holy Spirit, entering the throne room,
God's true praisers and worshipers.
So put on a garment of praise,
And lift the spirit of heaviness.
(Dedicated to Min. Lynch's Praise and Worship Team)

# STEPHANIE MATTHEWS – A MODERN DAY VIOLINIST

Captivated by classical music as a tender tot,
While casually viewing an educational tv show,
When suddenly appeared a man with violin and bow in hand,
A violinist named Maestro Pinchas Zuckerman.
She watched and she listened, putting down her toy,
And focused on the man playing the music her dad enjoys,
She waited till the end then ran and shared it with her dad,
Thus, begin her classical music journey
And her destiny with the violin.

She begin playing the violin at age four
And continued throughout her education.
Faced many tests and trials as a youth
While completing her musical training,
And even decided to give it up,
For a career in the sciences,
But God strengthened and encouraged her
Through family members and friends to persevere
And press forward to fulfill His purpose
And His vision for her life.

She completed her musical training at
Indiana U and Julliard too and chose not
To accept the call to enter
The Royal Conservatory in England.

When the season of musical training was completed,
She founded the Ebony Strings Quartet, and
StringCandy and helped develop the Alkali Ensemble.
As Stephanie's musical gift developed,
God opened doors, allowing her to perform
With orchestras, and string ensembles,
And travel to the five continents to perform
And conduct master classes.

God rewarded Stephanie for being obedient
And faithful with the gift that was given and put her
In the presence of Presidents, Bishops, heads of state
And royalty as well.
A winner of the National Symphony
Orchestra Young Soloist Competition,
And her name is etched in stone in the
Kennedy Center's History.
Now a violinist, composer, song writer,
Music director, and arts advocate.
She performs traditional classical, gospel,
Contemporary, and pop,
Writes music for gospel artists and pop artists alike,
Scores music for movie productions and film festivals,
Puts music to bible verses and poetry too,
And ministers to saints as they transition to glory.

Stephanie's musical gift was stirred up early in life,
She's developed it and invests it in the lives of others.
Her story is not over as you can see,
For eyes haven't seen nor ears heard the
Great things that God still has in store.
A Music Ambassador and a Joshua leader,

A light leading the way, blazing new paths
By living a faith-filled life,
Providing youth with an inspired life,
And showing them "with God all things
Are possible."

# DARIN ATWATER – SOULFUL SYMPHONY

At age four, music became a part of Darin's life,
As he sat creating music, moving his fingers
Across his grandmother's piano,
His loving mother exposed him to diverse genres
of music
Which built a solid foundation and love for it;

A church boy, influenced by gospel music,
Completed his musical training at an African
American University that grounded him in culture
and traditions,
Inspired and received revelation while reviewing
Romare Beardon's
Artistic works and envisioned what he must do.

A composer, conductor, pianist, and Ambassador for
the Arts,
Who redefined orchestral music and introduced it to
A broader cultural audience,
Captures the universal language of music through
voices and orchestral
Instruments, making it common ground for a diverse
culture,
Blending classical, gospel, spiritual, jazz, and hip-hop,
Appealing to the souls of a new audience of
music lovers.

A Joshua leader, and an Ambassador of Christ in the
Music Ministry,

Spreading the good news to the young and old,
To rejoice, clap one's hands and feet, feel the rhythm
of the music,
Just as it was meant to be.

A founder of the Soulful Symphony Orchestra
Which makes room for African Americans in
Orchestras.
He has been elevated by God and honored by men,
Named as one of the 30 leaders of the future by Ebony
Executive Leaders.
Darin's story is still being written, but do tell **his story,**
And praise God for giving the new generation
of youth,
An Ambassador of Music in the 21st Century
With fresh revelation and a fresh anointing,
And the audience a chance to use many of their
Senses as they engage and experience the music.

# REV. RICHARD SMALLWOOD – A MODERN DAY PSALMIST

The son of a pastor, and a beloved mother,
Possessed with the spirit of David,
Hummed melodies of hymns before words were
ever spoken,
Richard's musical gift was stirred up at an early age.

Began playing the piano by ear at five,
And received formal training at seven,
Thus becoming the pianist at his father's church.
Richard's mother nurtured his musical gift,
Exposing him to symphony concerts and clas-
sical music,
And he developed a love and passion for it.

Formed his first gospel group at age eleven,
Completed formal musical training at Howard
University,
And began blending classical, gospel, R&B, and pop,
Creating a unique sound of music.
His recordings are heard, bought and cherished
By both young and old.

A world class composer, pianist, arranger, singer,
Producer, and ordained minister.
Richard's musical gift has made room for him.
He formed the Richard Smallwood singers and has
Travelled throughout America, Europe, and Russia.
Honored by presidents, A Pope, and dignitaries
around the world.

Received numerous awards and high honors,
And inducted into the Gospel Music Hall of Fame.

Richard Smallwood is one of God's Modern Day
Psalmist,
Who knows he was chosen for this purpose for
a season,
And he's determined to spread the good news of Christ
Through this music until he makes his journey to his
Heavenly home in Glory.

# REV. ANDRAE CROUCH – THE FATHER OF MODERN GOSPEL

The father of modern gospel
Acquainted with an affliction,
Yet he walked in his musical calling
And ministered for half-a-century,
A ministry that spanned the U.S. and abroad.

Andrae's dad prayed to The Father above
Petitioning God to grant him the gift of music,
Thus, Andrae began his ministry of music
With his sister, Sandra, by his side.
A humble man whose music transcended racial lines.
A modern sound of gospel with cultural relevance,
That touched the lives of the young and old.
A legend who left an example for others to follow,
To create music that ministers to the spirit and soul
of youth.

A singer, songwriter, choir director and arranger,
Always giving God the glory for his gift,
And making Jesus His Lord and Saviour.
Focusing less on his affliction, but on doing the
will of God.
An Ambassador of Christ
Who helped spread the love of God through music
In the world
Influencing secular artists and entertainers too.

Now Andrae's time on earth has ceased,
And others have picked up the mantle

To carry on this great work
As Ambassadors in the Music Ministry,
Spreading the gospel with cultural relevance
To a new generation of believers.

# DR. RAYMOND JACKSON –
# CLASSICAL MUSIC AMBASSADOR

Born on American soil in Rhode Island,
An Ambassador of Christ in music and the Education
Kingdom,
A teacher, a mentor, an inspiration for generations
of youth.
Discovered and fulfilling his purpose during his
Season of time on Earth.

An example of a life that has developed his musical gift
That is used to bless others,
He showed youth how to achieve their God-given
purpose.
A disciplined and dedicated life for Christ,
That spans over half-a-century in music.
Completed his musical training at top music schools
In the U.S.A. and Europe.
An Ambassador of Christ whom God has allowed
To perform throughout America and Europe.

He founded a scholarship and mentoring program for
Gifted pre-college African American Pianists
To aid them in fulfilling God's calling.
Provides free piano lessons to poor children who have
musical gifts,
Re-introduced forgotten African descent composers
to the world.

God elevated him so others could see him lifted,
A living hope for a gifted nation of youth,

Who has been bestowed many honors,
First African American and musician inducted into
The Rhode Island Heritage Hall of Fame.
His life is a symbol of God's promise and reward to us
When we stir up our God-given gift,
Develop it, and use it to advance God's
kingdom agenda.
A servant of God who invests and sows
His talent and time in others for Christ.

# BISHOP JACKIE MCCULLOUGH – A PROPHETESS FOR THE NATIONS

Born on the Island of Jamaica to godly parents in
The gospel ministry,
But America became the family's new homeland.
Felt the call of God on her life as a teen,
Pursued her aspiration of becoming a medical doctor,
Trained and became a registered nurse,
Heard God's call again while in prayer on a
lunch break,
Thus, Jackie gave up nursing and obeyed God's call
And pursued His plan and purpose for her life.

Jackie began the Evangelism ministry
For college students, prisoners, the sick, and those
on the streets.
Angering the enemy, he attacked her family,
But God's grace was sufficient and carried her
through.
God found her faithful to His call on the home front,
And commanded her to go and fulfill the Great
Commission,
Of preaching and teaching to the nations of Africa,
Asia, Japan, U.S.A.,
And to her kindred in Jamaica for a season.
She matured spiritually, grew in great faith, filled
With the Holy Spirit, walking in holy boldness.

Evangelist McCullough established a Missionary
ministry

Providing medical treatment to her people on the Island.
Established a Christian college to train spiritual leaders For Christ.
As that season ended, Rev. McCullough
Founded an International Church to strengthen the faith
Of the local body of believers in New York.


A psalmist, an author, who preaches and teaches prophetic messages
From the uncompromised word of God,
With passion and conviction, compelling people
To believe it and receive it.
Upholding the word of God as a sword
And a mighty weapon to defeat and drive out the enemy!


God elevated her to the position of Bishop
To oversee His churches and to train spiritual leaders,
Who too would fulfill His plan and purpose,
Allowing the Kingdom of God to come on Earth.
A true shepherd who keeps watch over God's people,
And who continues to fulfill God's call
For her life as a humble servant on Earth.

# DR. MYLES MUNROE – A MODERN DAY APOSTLE

Born on an Island and grew up in an impover-
ished family,
But God gave him a dream of becoming "A
Transformative
Spiritual Leader" in the Kingdom of God on Earth.

At an early age, Myles gave his life, heart, and mind
to Christ.
Travelled to the U.S. to receive his spiritual and edu-
cational training,
That broadened his vision, mind, and view of
the world.
Interacted with White and Black Christians in the
Southern Bible Belt of Ameica,
Then returned home when his season of training ended.
The Holy Spirit was with Myles as he returned to his
homeland
To dispel the darkness that rested across the Island.
A light that burned brightly at home and abroad.

An ordained Apostle of the Lord Jesus Christ Who
influenced leaders
Of nations, Religions, Educational Institutions, and
businesses as well.
He imparted truths to believers through his teachings
and books.
Myles taught us how to expose and expel the reli-
gious yoke
And put on the Kingdom of God's yoke.

He taught believers around the world
To stir up within them their God-given gift,
"Allow it to be manifested upon the Earth in your life."
He told us that Jesus's teachings were
About the Kingdom of Heaven agenda.
Favored by God, the Heavenly Father and man,
Myles was honored by the Queen of England
And his government.

As he came to the end of his journey,
Myles's parting words to believers across the
World, like Paul, were " it is finished,
I have delivered to the world what I was born to do."
"I practiced what I preached."
He encouraged us to "stay faithful and focused,
Activate your God –given gift in your life,
God has made room for them in the world.
Take it to the world and remember God will be
With you," he said.
"So run the race that God has set before you."

# DR. MICHAEL YOUSSEF – CHRIST'S APOSTLE

A life endangered before birth,
Born to a poor Egyptian mother,
That God divinely intervened and saved,
And called while yet in his mother' womb.
Gave his life during teen years to Christ;
Had a childhood dream to leave Egypt
To become a citizen of the U.S.A.

Like the Israelites, God brought out of Egypt,
Into the promised land of Canaan, a land he dreamed of.
As life began to unfold, Michael heard God's call
And thus began his season of spiritual training.
God provided an open door to leave Egypt.
He journeyed to a foreign land to begin his training,
And chose a wife to walk by his side.

As the first phrase of training ended, God revealed
An open door to America and he entered in, continuing
On the path of spiritual training until that season ended.
Then God called him for a time as a World Evangelist
And Spiritual Leader.
Like the Apostle Paul, Michael walked humbly
Among the people of diverse races and cultures.
A faithful servant was he and God elevated him
To a position of authority, to impact the world
Through world leaders for Christ.

When the season ended, he proved faithful to
his calling
And God granted him his childhood dream of
Becoming a United State citizen.
Now the time had come to establish the Church of
the Apostles
And the World-Wide Evangelism Ministry,
A ministry that God has called him to.
Michael is prepared and fulfilling the Great
Commission
And a world vision of impacting the world for Christ,
Using modern technology, nation by nation.

# ARCHBISHOP DUNCAN WILLIAMS – A GIANT SLAYER

Born on the African continent
To African parents, and granted an unusual miracle.
The invisible hand of God rested upon him
Because God has a plan for his life
To live and impact nations;
Given the name "Nicolas" and as a teen
Relinquished his life to the Father above.
Then vowed to spread the gospel of Christ
To nations around the world.

A carrier of a distinct Apostolic anointing
Of prayer, healing, deliverance, and prophecy
To impact global churches and world leaders
In Africa, Asia, North America, and Europe.
A man acquainted with trials and tribulations,
But a man of great faith and a mighty prayer warrior.
A General in the army of the Lord,
And a spiritual giant of the Lord Jesus Christ,
Fulfilling "the Great Commission of spreading
The light and truth of Christ throughout the world."

The founder of the Global Prayer Summit,
Established a Missionary ministry to orphans
in Africa,
To minister to the motherless and fatherless.
The son of an Ambassador and Chief,
And an Ambassador of the Lord Jesus Christ.
Provides spiritual training to leaders in the Education
Kingdom,

And in the Media Kingdom to spread truth,
Not deception, to his beloved African people.
An author, a teacher, a servant leader,
Elevated and fashioned by God
And highly honored by men;

A voice to the nations,
Who still lives and walks in his divine calling,
As an Apostle and a champion for the Lord
Jesus Christ;
One who understands principalities, rulers of darkness,
Spiritual wickedness in high places,

Spiritual strongholds, and generational curses;
Accesses the supernatural power of God,
A true giant slayer and a light for the nations,
Impacting the world for Christ.
(A true giant slayer and a promise fulfilled to Bishop
Vinton R. Anderson)

# NELSON MANDELA – "KHULU"

A great South African General,
Who freed a nation of people –
The oppressed and the oppressors.
A moral guide, a human compass,
For all the world to see.

He dismantled and toppled
Racial dominance, triumphing over the media giant
And brought peace and victory to the African nation.
The Great Indian General Gandhi
Had gone before him,
And successfully defeated the oppressors,
The nonviolent – peaceful way,
But for General Mandela,
The African cry was sent out,
"Advance forward on the freedom fight!"

Much bloodshed and soldiers
Died on the battlefield,
Though captured and imprisoned,
The fight for justice and equality forged on,
At last, the Great General conquered
And defeated the oppressors,
With weapons of peace and nonviolence,
And gathered the people
For atonement and reconciliation,
And Freedom was finally won.

Now the world pays tribute
And honors this Great General,

Who, like Gandhi, left his mantle
Of leadership for other world leaders
To take up and fight the enemies
Of Justice and equality and freedom
Throughout the world.

# MUHAMMAD ALI – A COMPASSIONATE HUMANITARIAN

Witty and wise
Strong and unyielding
Fit and focused
Stood by his convictions
Walked in self respect
Courageous and radical
Poetic and charismatic
A shining star
A voice of peace
And free to be
Muhammad Ali.

# CORETTA "A CARRIER OF MARTIN'S DREAM"

A farmer's daughter acquainted with long walks,
Farm labor and racism,
An experience a child of the South can't escape.
A student, excellent in character, confidence,
and grace,
Who blossomed in gifts and abilities,
In the midst of a separate and unequal society.

As Coretta continued on the path of education,
God's plan for her life unfolded,
Her preparation in music prepared
Her to fulfill life's role on stage
As the wife of a Civil Rights Leader.

Coretta met her future husband,
Dr. Martin Luther King Jr.
The two united in marriage and Dr. King
Returned to the South
To answer God's call upon his life
And to fulfill his mission on Earth.

Side by side, Coretta marched
With Martin in the Civil Rights Movement.
She showed women all across the world
How to partner with their husbands
To fulfill his call and vision.

A carrier of Martin's dream,
Coretta continued the fight for economic justice

And human rights even when Martin's life ceased,
And God used her as a voice for International peace.

The King Center and a National Holiday
Were put in place to honor him,
To keep his legacy and dream alive
In the hearts and minds of future generations
Of African American boys and girls.

# PRESIDENT BARACK OBAMA – HOPE FOR A NATION

An uncommon name for an uncommon leader.
A 21st Century Charismatic leader of the Western World,
A name etched in history,
A U.S. President with international influence
Whose story will be told,
As the pages of history unfolds.

Barack Obama
A name written on the walls of public schools,
A name mothers are giving their new born sons;
A name uttered from the lips of children reading
Aloud their story books.

Barack Obama
The first African American President,
Who promotes international peace, not war,
A man with a multi-racial identity,
Well acquainted with racism in America,
Who understands the plight of the modern day
Pilgrims and immigrants.

Barack Obama
A man with a great vision
Who seized the American dream,
A mighty orator and Nobel Peace Prize Winner,
A man with great intellect and diplomacy
Who fought against internal struggles,
'Society's social ills and for people's civil rights,
And rose into a position of power and authority

To become a symbol of Hope
For a nation of people.

A compassionate leader who pardons prisoners,
And promotes reconciliation among nations;
A man who upholds government
By the people and for the people

And the rights for all American citizens,
And even instituted the Affordable Care Act,
A National Health Care Policy for all,
And his name is Barack Obama.

# MOTHER TERESA – "A SAINT"

Born in a family who knew no lack,
Raised by a loving mother,
And grew up in the Catholic Church.
Fascinated as a youth about stories of Missionary life.

Mother Teresa's soul was filled with the light of Christ
And His love for the human race.
When childhood ended and adult life began,
Mother Teresa left home to begin her missionary journey,
Never again seeing the face of her mother.

Far, far from home, like Jesus, she set out to do the Father's will.
Small in stature but grew mighty in spirit and faith,
With an unwavering commitment, self-discipline, and a prayer life.
She fulfilled her time of training and preparation to become a nun,
Thus began her service as "Sister Teresa."

Served wealthy female Indian youth until her missionary calling,
And gave up all comfort and took to the streets,
To minister to the poor, sick, and homeless,
All for the sake of Christ.
Like the little lad,
Mother Teresa opened her heart and hands
And gave God her life,
Becoming poor to enrich the lives of the poor.

She clothed herself with a white Indian garment (sari),
To honor the people she served.

Like a mustard seed, the Missionary of Charity spread
Across the world, serving the poor, sick, orphans, and
homeless.
Many hearts were touched and they took up the mission
Of caring for the poor, sick, and homeless too.

Mother Teresa's service spanned over half-a-century,
Until God called her home to glory.
Now many others have taken up these good works,
Following her example
To fulfill this missionary ministry and service to
the poor.

Many honors were bestowed upon Mother Teresa,
And the world stands amazed by her love and service
to humanity,
She has been elevated from sister, to mother, and now
a "Saint"
And God, the Father, has awarded her with a crown
And in heaven's hall of fame and a new name in glory
For living a selfish sacrificial life of love, service
to others,
And a consecrated life to Christ,
And her name will forever be read in the history pages
of life.

# An Intergenerational Legacy

# Contending for the Faith

## Flourishing Like Palm Trees

# A PRAYER FOR FUTURE GENERATIONS

Father in heaven above,
Guide the future generations in the world,
We've taught them your Holy Word,
About the Lord Jesus Christ and His love,
The ministry of angels and the Holy Spirit's job
on Earth.

We walked in faith and righteousness before them,
And showed them how to live this Christian life.
Teach them how to grow in grace in You
And in the knowledge of the Lord Jesus Christ.
Teach them how to live spirit-filled lives,
And expose and expel relational sins,
Daily abide in God's word, draw close to thee,
Then walk in truth, and they will be free.

Remind them as they continue their journey,
That they are not alone, to spread Christ's story,
And even though the god of this world seems
To be winning, OUR GOD IS STILL IN CONTROL!
You promise to always be there to see them through,
As they trust, obey, walk in faith, and love,"
And flourish until they too are called home to glory.

# AN E-MAIL MESSAGE

My Dearly Beloved,
As I enter into the golden years of my life, I envy not
the youth of today.
I am busy laying claim to every promise in prayer for
you. May God
Strengthen your faith to receive the abundant life that
Christ has provided for you.
Walk in authority as Ambassadors of Christ, upholding
the standards of God.
He loves you and Christ on the cross proves it. "Live
Holy lives!"
"Allow love to go the extra mile in you!" "Be indebted
to no one except to love." (Rom. 13:8)
Remember to "seek first the kingdom of God... ,"
(Mat. 6:33)
Engrave God's word on your hearts, live in the faith
zone, above see level,
Dress daily in God's armor, and fulfill your purpose
on Earth.


Finally, be led by the inward witness of your spirit
And keep in step with the Holy Spirit,
Use the word of God over your life to decree, declare
And command things in existence. Speak as if you are
The voice of God! May God deliver you from people
who call Him a liar!
Claim the truth and walk in it! Claim your position
and possessions in Christ, Eph. 2:6, Rom 8:17.
"Contend for the faith!" (Jude 1:3)
"Persevere with Christ!"

"May you flourish like palm trees!" (Ps. 92:12)
Remember to use your keys to the kingdom
Just as you have seen the elect do!
Much love and peace,
A Missionary in Christ

# KEEPERS OF THE LEGACY

Look to the Bright Morning Star, "Jesus,"
Make Him Savior, Lord, and Friend,
Receive the Holy Spirit,
Tell what God did for past generations,
Remembering that He's working miracles today,
Read God's word, meditate, pray, and praise,
Deposit your gift in the lives of men,
Always giving glory to God,
And commit to being keepers of the faith
And a godly legacy.

# A GOD MOTHER'S COMMANDMENTS

Love God with all your heart, soul, and strength,
and keep His commandments, (Mat. 22v37).

Be a spiritual mentor, and model a godly lifestyle.
Be committed to partner with your god child's parents
in his/her spiritual development.

Develop a close personal relationship and take the
time to see him/her as regularly as you can.
Listen and love and keep in communication with
your god child.
Provide wise counsel and guidance.
Pray for and with him/her regularly.

Provide educational support and cultural enrichment.
Become a cheerleader by celebrating major events
in his/her life.
Teach your god child about the world's governing
systems and its powers.

# A GOD FATHER'S COMMANDMENTS

Love God with all your heart, soul, and strength, and keep His commandments, (Mat. 22v37).

Be a spiritual mentor, and model a godly lifestyle.
Model a high moral character, excellent manners, and high standards of behavior.
Be committed to partner with your god child's parents in his/her spiritual development.

Develop a close personal relationship and take the time to see him/her as regularly as you can.
Listen and love and keep in communication with your god child.
Provide wise counsel and guidance.
Pray for and with him/her regularly.

Provide educational support and cultural enrichment.
Become a cheerleader by celebrating major events in his/her life.
Teach your god child about the world's governing systems and its powers.

# A GODLY GRANDMOTHER'S COMMANDMENTS

Love God with all your heart, soul, and strength, and be obedient to God's commandments, and hold God's word as the standard and authority for your life, (Mat. 22v37)

Model and teach a godly lifestyle and faith in action through everyday activities and living.

Teach God's standards and statues with love, grace, mercy, and patience.

Contribute to the educational training of the grandchildren.

Provide wise guidance and counsel to your grandchildren.

Pray for your grandchildren and PRAY WITH them.

Develop a loving personal relationship with your grandchildren.

Be willing to fulfill the role as parent when a family Crisis arises in the grandchild(ren)'s life/lives.

Teach the grandchildren good manners, modesty, and the spirit of hospitality.

Demonstrate a healthy lifestyle of good nutrition, Good health and good physical fitness.

Discipline your grandchildren with love. Allow them to experience the consequences of crossing God's boundaries.

Explain and share the rules and boundaries at your home with your grandchildren.

Teach them to obey and honor their parents in the Lord and God.

# A GODLY GRANDFATHER'S COMMANDMENTS

Love God with all your heart, soul, and strength, and be obedient to God's commandments and hold God's word as the standard and the authority for your life, (Mat. 22v 37).

Teach your grandchildren first by example and experience, and be a godly role model for them. Model Christian living through everyday activities and living.

Develop a loving personal relationship with your grandchildren.

Provide wise guidance and counsel.

Pray for your grandchildren and PRAY WITH them.

Teach God's standards and statutes with love, grace, mercy, and patience.

Discipline the grandchildren with love. Allow them to experience the consequences of crossing God's boundaries.

Contribute to the educational training of the grandchildren.

Explain and share the rules and boundaries at your home with your grandchildren.

Demonstrate a healthy lifestyle of good nutrition, good health, and good physical fitness.

Teach the grandchildren to honor and obey their parents in the Lord and God.

Teach your grandchildren about the world's governing systems and its powers.

# BLENDED FAMILY COMMANDMENTS

"Love One Another"

Make God the head of the marriage and center of the family.

Build your family on the foundation of the Lord Jesus Christ.

Develop a strong husband wife team, allowing the father to be the head, and the mother to be the heart of the family and home.

Build strong family relationships by serving, caring, sharing, and doing acts of kindness for each other.

Try to reach out and build good and positive relationships with ex-spouses, and allow the children opportunities to have ongoing healthy and nurturing relationships with parents and extended family.

Seek professional help to provide Christian counseling and support for the family.

Walk in love and forgiveness, speak life and blessings, uplift each other, encourage one another, and spend time together so the family members can bond together.

Parents should demonstrate love, trust, respect, honor, mutual agreement, compromise, reconciliation and restoration, and promote peace, unity, and harmony in the home.

Pray for the family and with the family (individually and together) in a circle and on your knees.

Parents should establish a set of family rules together and enforce them. Monitor appropriate language and music, modest apparel, good manners, school duties, chores, tech rules, and curfew hour.

Parents should establish rules for appropriate discipline for the younger and older children and seek Christian professional help for guidance and support. Discipline them in love.

Attend a Christ-centered bible believing local church together and fellowship with other believers. Provide spiritual training and educational training for the children. Study them to identify their gifting ( uniqueness and individuality), nurture, and help them to develop it.

Teach and train the children to work, be responsible, dependable, and productive members of the family and society. Help them to choose godly friends with these qualities.

Educate the children about worldly culture and governing systems ( politics, media, technology, music and language, movies, videos, games, dating, sex, gender id, and living together).

Teach the children how to manage their money (tithe and save).

Promote a healthy lifestyle, good nutrition, and good physical fitness for the family.

Take your family on vacations for recreational entertainment and relaxation.

# FROM A MOTHER TO HER DAUGHTER

(Preparation for Marriage)

What shall I say …
Or shall I begin this way?
My heart overflows
With joy for you!
As I witness a dream
And prayers come true.

A baby boy, the doctor said,
But the Lord revealed a shining pearl.
Who knew that God would send to me
A bouncing, precious baby girl!

A brand new life God gave to me
More precious than silver or gold.
I longed to hold my miracle,
To love, cherish, value, and mold.

I've sacrificed, prayed, and labored in love
Down through the years for you,
And now all grown up and graced with beauty
And womanhood … just look at you!

My love for you will never rest
I prayed God bless you with the best.
I didn't leave your life to fate,
But looked to God for your helpmate.

Today is your day
To wear your crown
And dress in a royal gown
To meet your prince in shining armor.
A day filled with family, friends, and formal.

As you come together
In love and life,
May God bless you,
As you embrace becoming
Husband and wife.

# FROM A FATHER TO HIS SON

(Preparation for Marriage)

My, has time gone by,
It seems like yesterday I brought you home
From the hospital,
I looked in awe upon my God-given miracle
Cuddled in my arms.
I've watched an energetic life filled
With wonder, curiosity, and adventure,
Running beside me as I held your tiny hand.
You grew, from grasping my legs to
Standing shoulder to shoulder beside me.
You grew, from babbling words to
Holding philosophical talks with me.

My, has time gone by,
You're getting married and it's just
Months away.
A man ...
Like me, you too have chosen a godly woman
To walk this journey with you.
My son, keep your promise to her,
Vow to love and be faithful to her.
Lead and she will follow, respect, and honor you,
And when you enter into the covenant on your wedding day,
Remember it's with God, your chosen wife, and you.

# WHEN OUR DAYS ARE OPPOSITE

How I long to commune with you
When I've had a wonderful day,
And everything has gone my way.
My spirit is lifted and I can't wait to celebrate,
But all too often I quickly forget,
That your day might have been the opposite of mine.

What if your day was bright and sunny,
And you experienced victory
Every step of the way,
And you couldn't wait to return home.
You stopped by the florist to pick up roses,
Even bought two tickets for a night at the movies ,
But when you arrived home I was sick in bed,
And could hardly raise my head.
What do you do when your day is the opposite
of mine?

What do we do when our lives are out of sync,
Disappointment and broken promises are all we see,
And negative words are passed between us,
Which makes matters worse.
Tell me, what do we do
When your day is the opposite of mine?

# THE BEAUTY OF YOU

When you smile
There's a twinkle in your eyes
I see the beauty of you.
Love radiates from you as
You place my hands in yours,
I hear the rhythmic beat of your heart
As I rest my head softly against your chest.

The smell of your aftershave and cologne
Stirs my emotions which gives fuel to my passion.
For I see the beauty of you
In the strength of your character
Your devotion to your family
The commitment to our marriage
Your dedication to a worthy cause
All put into action,
For I clearly see the beauty of you.

# LET'S GO DANCING TONIGHT

Hello my love, I just called to say
Let's go dancing tonight.
Put on your finest dress and dancing shoes.
Put away the bills, leave the dishes in the sink,
Postpone taking the clothes to the laundry,
Let's go dancing tonight
And have a groovy good time
And celebrate, just you and I.
Free your mind of worries and the stresses,
Grocery shopping can wait,
Spend the time grooming and dressing
But please don't be late.
Count the stars in the sky
Let's celebrate just you and I,
So let's go dancing tonight.

Oh baby, let's go dancing tonight,
And feel the rhythm of your heart beat
And your hands in mine.
Feel your warm embrace,
See the twinkle in your eyes
And your radiant smile,
And wave a banner of love over
The two of us.
Oh baby, let's get close,
I want to hear those three magic words
Whispered softly in my ear (" I love you"),
So let's go dancing tonight.

Let's get on our feet
And move to the rhythm of the beat.
You can follow my lead
As I guide you gently across the floor.

Let the music flow through us
And deepen our love tonight,
Come on baby,
Let's go dancing tonight.
 (Dedicated to Michael Matthews)

## LOVE THAT BINDS

Where true love abides,
It's felt in the rhythm of two hearts,
A dance in the soul of yours and mine,
A harmony in the spirits, and sparkles in the eyes,
A blaze within, a burst of joy, and a radiant smile,
A priceless gift of life,
And a miracle that remains forever a mystery.

# WHAT'S ON YOUR MIND?

What's on your mind?
…nothing you say,
But I can see your facial expression,
And read your body language,
So tell me, what's on your mind?

Are you trying to keep your thoughts inside,
And maintain your composure,
…afraid your emotions might give way
To a tidal wave of tears?
Can I offer you a cup of hot tea,
…care for a slice of lemon and a spoonful of sugar?
Come on, take a seat and rest your feet,
And tell me what's on your mind?

I promise, I'm not going anywhere,
My time is yours, let's just sit a while and chat,
I'll patiently give you a chance to speak,
If it takes all day, then I'll wait,
Until you tell me what's on your mind?

Let me take your hands in mine,
And look you straight in the eyes,
I can see a tear drop rest upon your cheek,
And a quiver upon your lips,
It's okay, release it, and let the tears flow,
I won't leave until you unburden your heart,
And verbally express your emotions,
You have a shoulder to lean on,
My ears are opened and clear to hear,
So speak, and tell me, "what's on your mind?"

# YOU CAN'T TAKE MY DREAM FROM ME

I thought you were my friend,
We've shared our hopes and secrets,
And I've even shared my diary too.
But you became jealous and wanted even more...
And began to say hurtful things to make me cry,
So it's time my friend to say good-bye,
Cause you can't take my dream from me.

I thought we were best of friends,
We've curled up in each other's bed
At our own slumber parties.
You've polished my nails and I've brushed your hair,
We sang and we danced and we've had so much joy.
We imagined being a bride maid at each other's
wedding,
But when I began to share my dream with you
You became jealous and wanted even more...
And started to say hurtful and painful things to
make me cry,
So it's time my friend for us to depart,
Cause you can't take my dream from me.

No, you can't take my dream from me,
I won't trade it, you can't buy it,
Cause it deep within my heart.
No, you can't take my dream from me,
I won't trade it, you can't buy it,
Cause it deep within my heart.

We have laughed and cried and have had many good times.
I've polished your nails and you've brushed my hair,
But when you began to say hurtful things to make me cry,
This is where I draw the line ,
Cause you can't have it, and I can't give it,
No, you can't take my dream from me,
No, no, no, you can't take my dream from me,
It's something that I cannot give,
Cause it's deep within my heart,
No, you can't take my dream from me.

# LEARN * RESPECT * ACHIEVE

I love to learn
At home and at school,
In the sunshine, rain or cold I rise,
And come to school each day
To listen to my teachers, oh yea, oh yea!
I walk and talk respect,
Talk and walk respect,
Walk and talk respect, oh yea, oh yea!
I study to achieve,
Do my homework and read,
Persevere to succeed,
And set my mind to achieve, oh yea, oh yea!
(Inspired by William Ramsay's Principal Dr. R. Casiano)

# BOOKS KINDLE A GIRL'S IMAGINATION

Just imagine…
Singing to the wind,
Floating on silvery clouds,
Sitting on a glowing rainbow,
And wearing sparkly stars in my hair.
Books take me places
I could never go
And let me be
What I could never be.

Just imagine…
Meeting the Frog Prince,
And blowing him a kiss,
Dancing at the knight's ball,
And laughing with Cinderella,
Galloping through the forest,
Rescuing Hansel, Gretel,
And Red Riding Hood's Granny.
Books take me places
I could never go
And let me be
What I could never be.

Just imagine…
Traveling around planet Earth,
On a tiny firefly,
Or soaring across the blue sky
On a dragonfly's wings,
Hidden in a whale's blowhole

Deep in the ocean,
And swimming beside friendly dolphins,
Or overlooking the horizon,
Standing in an eagle's nest.

Books take me places
I could never go
And let me be
What I could never be.

# BOOKS GIVE WINGS TO A BOY'S IMAGINATION

Books give wings to my imagination,
Letting me soar to many places,
I'm a knight dressed in armor,
Protecting the princess at the castle,
Racing with my buddies on motor bikes,
Attacking the enemy in an intergalactic fight.

Books give wings to my imagination,
Letting me soar to many places.
Frightened by the green dragon as
I pull the covers over my head,
I can hear the crowd cheering for
A champion and a basketball star.

Books for boys oh what a joy!
Letting my imagination travel- it's free!
Mom and dad are so proud I read,
They envision honors, crowns, college bound,
For a son who delights in reading books.

# 21ˢᵀ CENTURY HOUSE RULES

1. Protect and Care for Family Members
2. Attend Family Devotion, Family Prayer, Family Counsel
3. Speak the Truth Lovingly
4. Mind Your Manners, Show Hospitality, Watch Your Attitude
5. Respect Self and Others
6. Listen, Think, Speak, Communicate
7. Use Tongue and Words to Build Up Self/Others
8. Forgive, Love, A Hug A Day
9. Enjoy Being Together
10. The Family Eats Meals Around Dinner Table
11. Get Fit and Stay Fit
12. Parents Control Computer, Phone, TV/Radio, Entrances
13. Family Motto: Work, Study, Play
14. Obey Family Schedule, Curfew
15. Introduce Family to Friends
16. Complete House Chores, Maintain orderly Environment
17. Protect and Care for Family Pet(s)
18. Yell or Shout Only If There's Danger
19. Follow Emergency Plan – Fire Safety Plan
20. Train to Use First Aid Kit
21. Keep Active Batteries in Smoke /$CO_2$ Detectors

CPSIA information can be obtained
at www.ICGtesting.com
Printed in the USA
FFHW022007091118
49356491-53644FF